SEVERO ROSS

Fátima

Place of hope and peace

Edições Missões Consolata
Apartado 5
FÁTIMA-Portugal

The Consolata Missionaries

The first Consolata Missionaries came to Fatima in 1943, during the Second World War. Warmly welcomed by the religious authorities and the local people as the «Missionaries of Our Lady», in the following year they opened up, at a short distance from the Sanctuary, a seminary for the formation of future Missionaries. Meanwhile, Fr. John De Marchi, having gathered information about the apparitions directly from the living witnesses of the locality, published a book entitled «A Lady brighter than the sun», which was widely diffused and translated into various languages. The English edition was reprinted in 1980, under the title of «Fatima from the beginning».

The Consolata Institute was founded in 1901 by Fr. Joseph Allamano, a contemporary of St. John Bosco and nephew of St. Joseph Cafasso, during his time as Rector of the Sanctuary of Our Lady of Consolata in Turin, Italy.

At the present time, Consolata Missionaries are working in six African countries - Ethiopia, Kenya, Tanzania, Mozambique, Republic of South Africa and Zaire, and in four of Latin America - Argentine, Colombia, Brazil and Venezuela. There are seminaries in Italy, Spain, Portugal, Ireland, United States, Canada, and in some mission lands.

In 1910, Fr. Joseph Allamano founded the Consolata Missionary Sisters who are presently working in different countries of Europe, Africa and the Americas.

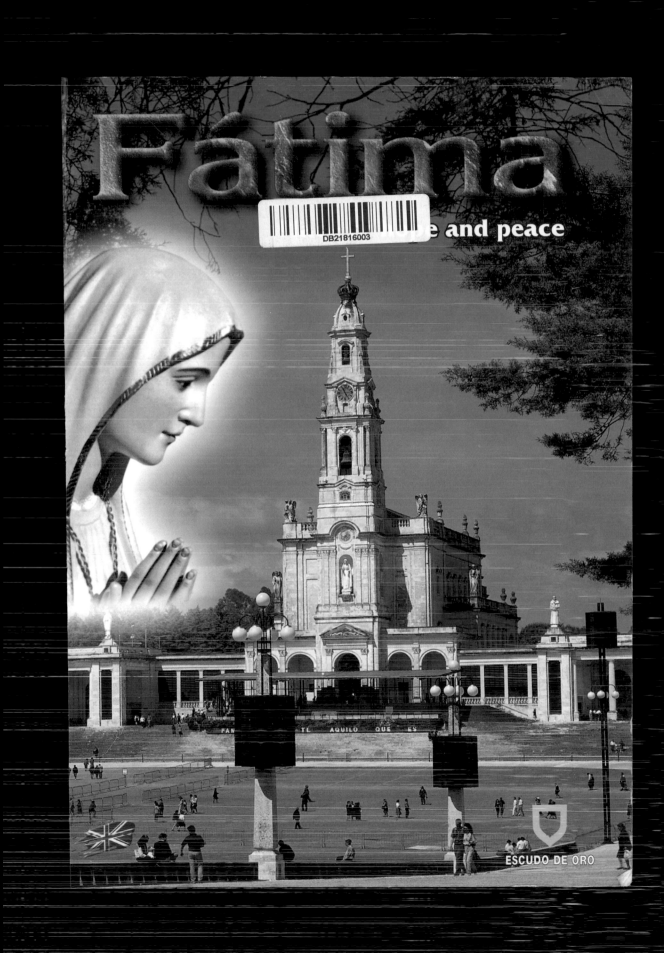

Fátima

hope and peace

ESCUDO DE ORO

Panorama of Fatima and the Cova da Iria.

Brothers and Sisters,

Devote your attention to this book, for it may change the direction of your life. The pictures within it and the message it brings you are not only among the most evocative, but above all, the most penetrating of the many you may have seen and heard in the course of your travels and pilgrimages.

The unique characteristic of Fatima lies in the fact that here we have the Gospel as God announces it to us today for this century in which we live: a century of invention, discovery and enthusiasm, but also a century of sin. It recalls the great moment of which Genesis speaks: God created man, man discovered the universe, and the serpent tempted man to declare himself equal to God and refuse to give due praise to the Creator, crying out: «I will not serve».

Today, as then, the Lord God comes down to man's lost paradise, and offers him once again the good news of salvation.

Men of the twentieth century, redeemed by Jesus Christ, have fallen into atheism, intoxicated as they are by new discoveries and the ever present snares of the infernal serpent. Their reason is shackled and their hearts are empty. But at Fatima they hear the announcement of God's great victory: «In the end my Immaculate Heart will triumph» This prophecy is a promise of Mary, Mother of the Church who, when she visited Fatima, came to repeat the «Magnificat» of her first visitation as Mother of the Saviour.

Brothers and Sisters, do you now understand how you can leave Fatima with a new direction to your life? It is because the Heart of your Mother brought you here, and the grace of Fatima is conversion of heart.

May your Guardian Angel pray with you!
May your Mother's smile ever shine on you!
To the glory of God the Almighty, Father, Son and Holy Spirit!

Father Luciano Guerra
Rector of the Sanctuary of Fatima

FATIMA

Fatima, in the very heart of Portugal, is located in the mountainous central region of the Serra de Aire, about thirty miles from the Atlantic Ocean. Originally a remote village in the municipality of Vila Nova de Ourém, it now enjoys the status of a town. Such place names, like so many others in Portugal, go back to Moorish times. Fatima was the name of the daughter of Mahomet, the great prophet of Islam.

About half a mile from Fatima parish church lies the little hamlet of Aljustrel, where the three little shepherds were born, to whom Our Lady appeared from May to October in 1917. To the west of Aljustrel, on a hillside covered with olive trees, there is a small rocky mound known as the Loca do Cabeço, where the angel appeared to the three little shepherds on two different occasions.

Over a mile to the west lies the Cova da Iria, one of the many undulating valleys of the region. It is here that Our Lady appeared five times to the little shepherds. In another small valley, on the hillside between Aljustrel and Loca do Cabeço, lies the Valinhos, where Our Lady appeared to them on the 19th of August, 1917.

Fatima, fount of hope

WARS, ATHEISM, HATRED OF RELIGION

The years 1916 and 1917 will be remembered as among the darkest in the history of the peoples of Europe.

The major powers were ferociously tearing one another asunder in a great fratricidal war- the First World War - which was to cause the death of millions of victims.

In 1917, the Bolshevik Revolution broke out in Russia. As time went by, it was to bring to many nations, and even impose by force, the principles of atheism, religious persecution and the negation of the spiritual values of the human person. At that very time, in Fatima, the Angel of Peace and the Virgin Mother of God and of men, brought to the three little shepherds a message of peace, of hope and of love for all mankind.

Portugal, a small nation of but fifty thousand square miles and less than ten million inhabitants, lies to the west of Spain, facing the Atlantic Ocean. Portuguese independence dates from 1139, the year of its decisive victory over the Moors. As a seafaring people and a nation of explorers, Portugal was among the first to venture on the ocean highways towards the discovery of unknown lands, bringing them what was good and what was bad in European civilization of those times.

In 1917, Portugal found itself in a desperate condition, politically, socially and economically. Governments followed one another, all equally unable to solve the nation's problems. Revolutions were the order of the day, and the people lost all confidence in their rulers. In the economic field, there was complete bankruptcy; on the military plane, war was being waged on two fronts - in France and in the African colonies.

The population of Portugal at that period consisted mainly of humble country folk, honest and hard-working people even if poor in material goods. Where religion

Partial view of the Basilica and colonnade.

Detail of the monument of the apparition of the Angel.

Group in marble erected in 1958 on the Cabeço, a hillside near Fatima, in memory of the first and third apparition of the Angel.

Lucia: the eldest, was born on the 22nd of March, 1907. Dark complexioned, with eyes black and shining under heavy eyebrows, she had dark hair, a slightly flattened nose, thick lips and a wide mouth. She was endowed with an excellent temperament, with a sweet and lively disposition. She was especially fond of children, and they in turn loved her dearly.

Francisco: Lucia's cousin, was born on the 11th of June, 1908. His face was plump and round, his mouth small, and he was well built. Affable and peaceable by nature, he loved games and spent hours playing his flute. He was a born lover of nature.

Jacinta: Francisco's sister, was born on the 11th of March, 1910. She had a shapely little body, a wellrounded face, bright eyes, thin lips, a small chin, and a lovely expression. She was by nature unusually sensitive. She was attached to Lucia by an intensely tender and deep friendship.

She was incapable of telling a lie even in the most trifling matters, and held that the truth must be told, even at the cost of sacrifice. She loved sheep, little lambs, flowers, the stars, the moon which she called Our Lady's Lamp, and the whole of nature. She had a passion for dancing. At times she manifested a certain wilfulness. She loved to pray.

These children, in no wise different from others, and who had received from their parents a good sound education in the christian faith, were to be chosen as the messengers of the good news of Fatima to a world without love, without hope and without peace.

was concerned, those in power endeavoured to stir up hatred and persecution of the Church. As far back as 1911, Alfonso Costa, then Head of State, approved the law of total separation of the Church and State in the following declaration: «Thanks to this law, Portugal, within two generations, will have succeeded in completely eliminating Catholicism». Schoolchildren were obliged to march through the streets, carrying banners inscribed with the words: «Neither God, nor Religion».

THE THREE LITTLE SHEPHERDS

There are many passages in the Gospel, in which the virtue of humility is shown to be essential if we are to please God. Our Lady of Fatima stressed this aspect when she chose three humble shepherd children to transmit her message to the world. They were three perfectly normal children, in no way different from any of their companions, and their sole concern was to take the family flocks out to pasture.

THE APPARITIONS OF THE ANGEL, «HERALD OF THE VIRGIN»

In the history of Israel, God's chosen people, and in the history of the Church, the Lord has frequently sent his angels as bearers of good tidings that would give men a better understanding of His word and His will.

At Fatima in 1916, a year before the Apparitions of the Mother of God, an Angel came three times to visit the little shepherds. As Our Lady's messenger, and forerunner of still greater happenings to come, the Angel prepared the little seers towards a greater understanding, living and spreading of Our Lady's message, which was none other than that of the Gospel.

First Apparition

The first apparition of the Angel took place in the spring of 1916 (the seers could not recall the exact date), on a rocky hillside near Aljustrel called Loca do Cabeço. It was a rainy day, and the three little shepherds, Lucia, Francisco and Jacinta, had sought shelter among the rocks. When the sky cleared, they stayed in the same spot, enjoying their games.

Suddenly, they beheld a strange light coming towards them from the east. When it drew near, they saw that it was «a young man, about fourteen or fifteen years old, whiter than snow, transparent as crystal when the sun shines through it, and of great beauty» (Lucia's Memoirs).

He drew closer and said: «Do not be afraid! I am the Angel of Peace. Pray with me.».

Kneeling on the ground, he bowed down until his forehead touched the ground, and asked them to pray with him three times the following prayer:

«My God, I believe, I adore, I hope and I love You! I ask pardon of You for those who do not believe, do not adore, do not hope and do not love You.»

Then, rising, he said: «Pray thus. The Hearts of Jesus and Mary are attentive to the voice of your supplications.» Then he disappeared.

During the whole of that day, and the following day too, the three little shepherds were so immersed in the presence of God that they were unable to speak, even among themselves.

Second Apparition

This took place two months later, in the summer of 1916, when the little shepherds were playing near the well behind Lucia's house. Suddenly the same Angel appeared to them and said:

«What are you doing? Pray! Pray very much! The Hearts of Jesus and Mary have designs of mercy on you. Offer prayers and sacrifices constantly to the Most High.»

«How are we to make sacrifices?» Lucia asked.

«Make of everything you can a sacrifice, and offer it to God as an act of reparation for the sins by which He is offended, and in supplication for the conversion of sinners.»

The words were indelibly impressed upon the minds of the three little shepherds. From then on, they frequently recited the prayer which the Angel had taught them at the first Apparition, and began to offer many sacrifices to God.

On the right: the Statue of Our Lady of Fatima in the Chapel of the Apparitions.

Below: the Sanctuary with the little Chapel of the Apparitions, which marks the spot where Our Lady appeared to the three little shepherds.

Nothing remains of the holmoak tree on which Our Lady stood; every bit has long since be taken away by pilgrims as a precious relic.

Third Apparition

In the autumn of the same year 1916, the little shepherds were up on the slopes of the Loca do Cabeço, where the Angel had appeared to them for the first time. The children were prostrate on the ground, saying the prayer that the Angel had taught them, when an extraordinary light shone upon them. They looked up, and beheld the Angel. He was holding a chalice in his left hand, with a host suspended above it, from which some drops of blood fell into the chalice. Leaving the chalice and the host suspended in the air, the Angel prostrated beside the little shepherds and asked them to say the following prayer:

«Most Holy Trinity, Father, Son and Holy Spirit, I adore You profoundly, and I offer You the most precious Body, Blood, Soul and Divinity of Jesus Christ, present in all the tabernacles of the world, in reparation for the outrages, sacrileges and indifference with which He Himself is offended. And, through the infinite merits of His most Sacred Heart, and the Immaculate Heart of Mary, I beg of You the conversion of poor sinners».

Then, rising, the Angel took the chalice and the host in his hands. He gave the host to Lucia, and the contents of the chalice to Francisco and Jacinta, saying as he did so: «Take and drink the Body and Blood of Jesus Christ, horribly outraged by ungrateful men. Make reparation for their crimes and console your God».

Once again, he prostrated on the ground and repeated with them, three times more, the same prayer «Most Holy Trinity...». He then disappeared. He had completed his mission.

Six months later, the heavens would open once more to make way for her who was to bring a message of love and salvation to mankind.

THE APPARITIONS OF OUR LADY

First Apparition

13th of May

Sunday, the 13th of May, 1917, was a beautiful day of sunshine and blue skies. After Mass, the three little shepherds, carrying their lunchbags, set out with their flocks for the Cova da Iria, a small semicircular valley about a mile and a half from Aljustrel . While the sheep were peacefully grazing, the children ate their lunch and then began to play. Lucia herself tells us:

«Suddenly, we saw what seemed to be a flash of lightning. We decided that we had better go home. Hurrying towards the road with our flocks, we were only half way down the slope when we saw another flash. We had only gone a few steps further when, there before us on a small holmoak, we beheld a Lady all dressed in white. She was more brilliant than the sun, and radiated a light more clear and intense than a crystal glass filled with sparkling water, when the rays of the burning sun shine through it». Then Our Lady spoke to them:

«Do not be afraid. I will do you no harm».

«Where are you from?» asked Lucia, speaking for all three of them.

«I am from heaven».

«What do you want of me?» Lucia asked eagerly.

«I have come to ask you to come here for six months in succession, on the 13th day, at this same hour. Later on, I will tell you who I am and what I want».

After a little while, the Lady continued:

«Are you willing to offer yourselves to God and bear all the sufferings He wills to send you, as an act of reparation for the sins by which He is offended, and of supplication for the conversion of sinners?»

«Yes, we are willing, replied Lucia earnestly, in the name of all three of them. «Then you are going to have much to suffer, but the grace of God will be your comfort».

Finally, the Lady in white said:

«Pray the Rosary every day, in order to obtain peace for the world and the end of the war».

«Then», Lucia tells us, «Our Lady began to rise serenely, going up towards the east, until she finally disappeared in the immensity of space. The light that surrounded her seemed to open up a path before her in the firmament».

The children remained, spellbound, gazing at the heavens. Returning to themselves, they spent the rest of the day in the Cova da Iria. They agreed to say nothing to anyone about what had happened. In spite of this agreement, the youngest of the three, Jacinta, who was only seven years old, kept exclaiming: «Oh, what a beautiful Lady!» That same evening she revealed the secret to her mother. This was the beginning, both for the children and for their families, of that long period of humiliation and suffering which Our Lady had foretold. The people did not believe in them, and were not slow to scoff at them.

Statue of Our Lady of Fatima venerated since many years in the Basilica.

Arriving of pilgrims in the Sanctuary. Scenes of everyday occurrence in Fatima, especially during the summer months.

The Statue of Our Lady venerated in the Chapel of the Apparitions.

Second Apparition

13th of June

News of the May apparition quickly spread throughout the parish of Fatima. Few people accepted it, and the little shepherds began to be badly treated. Despite this, the 13th of June, feast of St. Anthony of Lisbon, patron saint of Portugal, brought about fifty people to the Cova da Iria. The Lady in white appeared, just as she had promised. «I wish you to come here on the 13th of next month, to pray the Rosary every day..»

She then promised to take Francisco and Jacinta to heaven very soon.

«But you», she said to Lucia, «are to stay here some time longer. Jesus wishes to make use of you to make me known and loved. He wants to establish in the world devotion to my Immaculate Heart».

«Am I to stay here alone? she asked sadly.

«No, my daughter. Don't lose heart. I will never forsake you. My Immaculate Heart will be your refuge and the way that will lead you to God».

Then she opened her hands. «In front of the palm of Our Lady's right hand», Lucia tells us, «was a heart encircled by thorns which pierced it. We understood that this was the Immaculate Heart of Mary, outraged by the sins of humanity, and seeking reparation».

Pilgrims on the way to Fatima. Many of them arrive after having walked hundreds of kilometres.

Third Apparition

13th of July

When the 13th of July arrived, the little shepherds had to overcome much opposition on the part of their families. Some said that it was the work of the devil, and others that it was an invention of hell.

But when the Lady from heaven came to speak for the third time to her three little friends, she said: «Continue to pray the Rosary every day in honour of Our Lady of the Rosary, in order to obtain peace for the world and the end of the war, because only she can help you».

Lucia asked her to work a miracle so that everybody would believe that she was appearing to them. «In October, I will tell you who I am and what I want, and I will perform a miracle for all to see and believe».

Overjoyed, and without further ado, Lucia presented to the Lady the requests of various persons in need, for the most part graces of healing and conversion. The Lady replied that it was necessary for such people to pray the Rosary in order to obtain these graces. And she continued: «Sacrifice yourselves for sinners, and say many times, especially whenever you make some sacrifice: O Jesus, it is for love of You, for the conversion of sinners, and in reparation for the sins committed against the Immaculate Heart of Mary». Then, Lucia tells us, Our

Lady opened her hands and the little shepherds beheld a most terrifying vision. They saw hell and, within it, the demons and the souls of the damned. The children grew pale as death, as several witnesses have assured us. It was at that moment that Lucia cried out: «Oh, Our Lady!» Terrified, and as if to plead for succour, the children looked up at Our Lady, who said to them so kindly and so sadly:

«You have seen hell where the souls of poor sinners go. To save them, God wishes to establish in the world devotion to my Immaculate Heart. If what I say to you is done, many souls will be saved and there will be peace. The war is going to end; but if people do not cease offending God, a worse one will break out.

Pilgrims at prayer. Some of them cross the entire square on their knees, praying the rosary.

«When you see a night illumined by an unknown light, know that this is the great sign given you by God that He is about to punish the world for its crimes, by means of war, famine and persecutions of the Church and of the Holy Father. To prevent this, I shall come to ask for the consecration of Russia to my Immaculate Heart, and the Communion of Reparation on the First Saturdays. If my requests are heeded, Russia will be converted, and there will be peace; if not, she will spread her errors throughout the world, causing wars and persecutions of the Church. The good will be martyred, the Holy Father will have much to suffer, various nations will be annihilated. In the end, my Immaculate Heart will triumph. The Holy Father will consecrate Russia to me, and she will be converted, and a period of peace will be granted to the world... Do not tell this to anybody».

The vision of hell, and the prophecies concerning Russia and the uncertain future of the world, constitute the first two parts of the secret of Fatima, a secret which was to be the cause of much suffering to the little seers.

Finally, Our Lady said: «When you pray the Rosary, say after each mystery: O my Jesus, forgive us, save us from the fire of hell. Lead all souls to heaven, especially those who are most in need».

Fourth Apparition

19th of August

Even the newspapers had begun to take an interest in the Fatima apparitions. They took the authorities to task for their negligence and inefficiency in failing to put a stop to the «farce» of the Cova da Iria.

Feeling that this attack was aimed at himself, the Administrator of Vila Nova de Ourém decided to have recourse to a stratagem.

On the morning of the 13th of August, feigning a desire of being present at the apparition, he invited the three little shepherds into his carriage. But, instead of taking them to the Cova da Iria he turned about and set off at full speed for the Town Hall at Vila Nova de Ourém. There, the little shepherds, individually and together, were subjected to severe questioning, and were threatened with torture and a terrible death: «We shall throw you into a cauldron of boiling oil». All this was to induce them to deny the tales they had spread abroad. The children refused to be intimidated and persisted in their decision to say nothing. On the 15th of August they were taken back home.

On the 19th of August, still feeling very sad because they had been unable to keep their appointment with Our Lady, the little shepherds set out to pasture their flocks in a place called Valinhos. Suddenly, they noticed the signs which usually preceded an apparition. The brightness of the sun faded and the air grew cooler, and they saw the flash of light which they called lightning.

Our Lady appeared, standing on a holmoak. She renewed her promise to perform a miracle in October «so that all may believe». Our Lady also spoke of having a chapel built in the Cova da Iria. Finally, she said: «Pray, pray very much, and make sacrifices for sinners; for many souls go to hell, because there are none to sacrifice themselves and to pray for them».

And she began to ascend as usual towards the east. From then on, Our Lady's request that they should make sacrifices for sinners was constantly present to the mind of the little shepherds, and increased their thirst for making sacrifices. They gave away their

The Sanctuary during the Candlelight Procession.

The statue of Our Lady carried in procession.

lunch, and gave up drinking water even on the hottest days of summer. They went so far as to tie a rope tightly round their waists in order to suffer all the more; Francisco and Jacinta continued to wear the rope even during the illnesses which were to lead to their death.

Fifth Apparition

13th of September

While, on the one hand, there were many who had made every effort to put a stop to the «farce» of the Cova da Iria, on the other hand, the number of those who believed in the apparitions was growing rapidly. Thus, on the 13th of September, about 25,000 people were present for the appointment with Our Lady.

«What do you want of me? asked Lucia, as usual. «Continue to pray the Rosary», Our Lady said, «in order to obtain the end of the war... In October, I will perform a miracle so that all may believe». Between the 13th of September and the 13th of October, life became more and more difficult for the little shepherds. Politicians and the enemies of religion were already savouring in advance the grand finale of what they considered to be a farce. Besides this, in Aljustrel itself where the children lived, the majority of the people were disbelieving and hostile. Priests, and members of their own families, tried to persuade the little seers to admit that they had lied. Others had recourse to threats. Early in the morning on the 12th of October, Lucia's mother awakened her daughter with these words: «Oh Lucia, we had better go to confession. They say that we are going to die tomorrow in the Cova da Iria. If the Lady does not perform the miracle, the people will kill us. It would be best for us to go to confession so as to be prepared for death». «Mother, if you want to go to confession, Lucia replied calmly, «I'll go too, but not for that reason. I'm not afraid. I'm absolutely certain that tomorrow the Lady will do everything she has promised».

A priest, after speaking to the little shepherds, was very worried and gave this advice: «The best thing to do would be to send telegrams in every direction, saying that it is all a made-up story».

Sixth Apparition

13th of October

On that day, about 70,000 people were present in the Cova da Iria - the devout, the curious, unbelievers, atheists, as well as journalists who had come solely with the express purpose of «unmasking the hoax». Everyone was soaked from the rain that fell continuously right up to the moment of the apparition. Lucia's mother, with tears running down her cheeks, walked beside her daughter, saying: «If my daughter is going to die,

The big square during the weekly pilgrimage.

Solemn ceremonies of the monthly pilgrimage on the 13th. From May to October the number of participating pilgrims reaches gigantic proportions.

I want to die at her side». The long wait was becoming wearisome, when, at midday, Lucia cried out: «Silence! Be quiet! Our Lady is coming!» At that instant, the seer became oblivious of everything around her. «What do you want of me?» she asked for the last time. «I want to tell you that a chapel is to be built here in my honour. I am the Lady of the Rosary. Continue always to pray the Rosary every day. The war is going to end».

Lucia then presented to Our Lady the requests of a great number of people. «Some yes, but not others», replied Our Lady. «They must amend their lives and ask forgiveness for their sins». Looking very sad, Our Lady said: «Do not offend the Lord our God any more, because He is already so much offended». As Our Lady parted from her three little friends for the last time, she opened her hands and made them reflect on the sun. As she ascended, the reflection of her own light continued to be projected on the sun itself. Indeed, Our Lady shone more brightly than the sun. The little shepherds then beheld other visions near the sun: Saint Joseph with the Child Jesus blessing the world, with Our Lady; Jesus blessing the world, and Our Lady of Dolours; and lastly Our Lady of Carmel.

Meanwhile, Lucia had suddenly cried out: «Look at the sun!». The multitude then beheld what was afterwards called the Miracle of the Sun. Here is the testimony of Avelino de Almeida, special

The Basilica seen from the Colonnade.

Moment of the solemn Eucharistic Concelebration on the main altar.

reporter for the anti-clerical daily «O Seculo»: «The sun looked like a plaque of dull silver, and it was possible to look at it without the least discomfort. It neither burned nor blinded the eyes. It might have been an eclipse which was taking place. But at that moment a great shout went up, and one could hear the spectators nearest at hand shouting: 'A miracle! A miracle! A marvel! A marvel!'». Before the astonished eyes of the crowd, whose aspect was biblical, as they stood bareheaded and pallid with fear eagerly searching the sky, the sun trembled, made sudden incredible movements outside all cosmic laws - the sun 'danced', according to the typical expression of the people». Jacinta's

father, Ti Marto, recalls: «All eyes were fixed on the sky when, at a certain moment, the sun seemed to stop, and then begin to move and dance. It stood still, then began to dance once more, until it seemed that it was being detached from the sky and was falling upon us. It was a terrible moment!». Many cried out: «O Jesus! We are all going to die!». Others pleaded: «Our Lady, help us!». There were some people who confessed their sins out loud. Finally, the sun stood still in its usual place. One last inexplicable marvel - all those people who had been drenched by the rain were suddenly completely dry! The Fatima apparitions had come to an end.

Annual International Children's Pilgrimage, always on the 10th of June.

A bishop in prayer.

On the right: Offering of the wheat during the pilgrimage on the 13th of August.

Below: Procession of pilgrims bringing the pyxes full of Hosts to the altar, during a Mass on the 13th.

General view of the big square full of pilgrims during the Mass on the 13th of May.

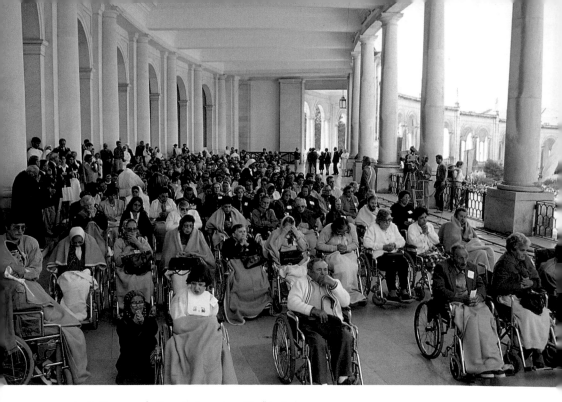

In Fatima as well as in Lourdes, liturgical acts and special prayers are reserved to the sick.

Below: Blessing of the sick.

Farewell procession: after hl. Mass the statue of Our Lady is brought back to the chapel of the apparitions.

The precious crown, which the statue of
Our Lady wears only on the days 12-13,
has been offered by Portuguese women.
It is all of gold and weighs 1.200 grams;
313 pearls and 2.679 precious stones
embellish it. In the middle has been
inserted the bullet, offered by Pope John
Paul II, to proof that Our Lady of Fatima
had protected him in the attempt on the
13th of May 1981 in Rome.

The statue of Our Lady in front of the
Chapel of the Apparitions.

An enormous multitude of pilgrims takes leave of Our Lady, waving white handkerchiefs.

Beside: two solemn moments of the visit of the Holy Father.
Above: Meeting with the priests and religious in the centre Paul VI.
Below: Vigil on the big square, with participation of a multitude of pilgrims.

On this page: The Holy Father in prayer before the statue of Our Lady, and with Sr. Lucia, the only survivor from the three little shepherds.

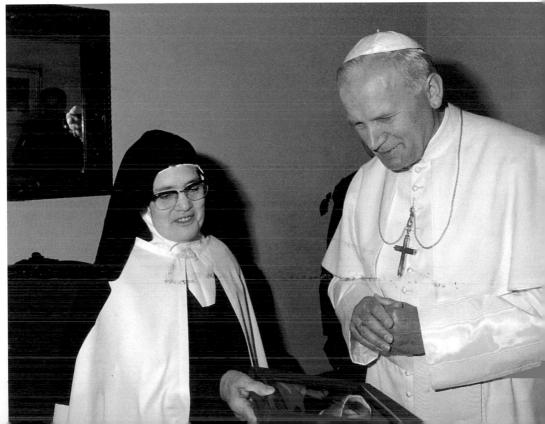

Interior of the Basilica and stained glass windows, one depicting Lucia and Jacinta scattering flowers during a Corpus Christi procession, the other recording the third apparition of the Angel.

Painting in the centre of the Apse, giving a general idea of the apparitions and their approval by the ecclesiastical authorities. ▷

Detail of the Sanctuary portico with the stations of the Cross.

JESVS ENCONTRA SVA MÃE SANTISSIMA

Interior of the adoration chapel, where the Blessed Sacrament remains exposed day and night, in accordance with the message of Fatima requiring prayer and reparation.

Front of the Basilica with the monument of the Sacred Heart of Jesus.

Details of the way which the little shepherds took, and where you find the Way of the Cross, constructed with gifts of the Hungarian people, in memory of what happened in Budapest in 1956.

The chapel erected in the Valinhos locality, in memory of the fourth apparition of Our Lady on the 19th of August, 1917.

Some stations of the Way of the Cross on the way to Valinhos.

The Calvary constructed on the place where ends the Way of the Cross, and the Chapel of St. Stephen, King of Hungaria.

Below: The interior of the Chapel of St. Stephen.

The three little shepherds

Francisco

He was born on the 11th of June, 1908, son of Manuel Marto and of Olimpia de Jesus. He was Jacinta's brother and Lucia's cousin. During the apparitions of the Angel and of Our Lady, he could see everything but could hear nothing. Lucia and Jacinta told him -what the Angel and Our Lady had said. When, in the first apparition, Lucia asked Our Lady if Francisco would go to heaven, Our Lady replied: «Yes, he will go there too, but he must say many Rosaries». Francisco, convinced that Our Lady would come for him very soon, showed little interest in attending school. On the way there, he often said to Lucia and Jacinta: «You go on. I'll go into the church to keep the Hidden Jesus company». Many witnesses testified that they had received great graces after having asked Francisco to pray for them. Francisco fell sick in October 1918. To those of his family who assured him that he would soon get better, Francisco would promptly reply: «It is no use. Our Lady wants me in heaven with her!» As the illness grew worse, Francisco continued offering sacrifices to console Jesus who was offended by so many sins. «I am suffering a lot», he would say to Lucia, «but never mind! I suffer everything for love of Jesus and Our Lady. I would like to suffer more, but I am unable to do so!». «Mother, I no longer have the strength to say the Rosary out loud. When I try to pray the Hail Mary, I can't keep my mind on it any more». «Father, I want to receive Jesus in Holy Communion before I die! (He had not yet made his First Communion). He wished first to make his confession. He called Lucia and Jacinta and asked them if they could recall any sins which he had committed. His cousin and his sister could only remember some minor misdeeds. Francisco burst into tears and said: «I have already confessed those sins, but I'll do so again. Maybe it is because of these sins which I committed that Jesus is so sad! Would you also ask Our Lord to forgive me my sins.» Soon afterwards, for the first (and last) time, he encountered the Hidden Jesus in the Sacred Host. When he was no longer able to pray, he asked his cousin Lucia and his sister Jacinta to pray the Rosary aloud, so that he could accompany them in his heart. On the last morning of his life, he once again asked pardon of his family for all his faults. Then he said to his mother: «Look, mother, do you see that beautiful light over there by the door?» It was the 4th of April, 1919. At ten o'clock in the morning, as the sun shone brightly into his small and humble room, Francisco departed for heaven to be forever with «his Lady», whose beauty had so won his heart. He was laid to rest in a simple grave in the parish cemetery. On the 12th of March, 1952, the mortal remains of the little seer were translated to the side-chapel on the right hand side of the high altar in the Basilica.

Jacinta

She was born on the 11 th of March, 1910, daughter of Manuel Marto and Olimpia de Jesus. She was Francisco's

The parish church of Fatima, where the three little shepherds have been baptized.

sister and Lucia's cousin. At the time of the apparitions of the Angel, she was only six years old. She was the youngest of the little seers. During the apparitions she saw and heard everything, but she never spoke either to the Angel or to Our Lady. Being intelligent and very sensitive, she was profoundly impressed when she heard Our Lady say: «The Lord our God is already so much offended», and

The parents of Francisco and Jacinta, Manuel Marto and Olimpia de Jesus.

on another occasion: «Pray, pray very much, and make sacrifices for sinners». After the vision of hell, she decided to offer herself completely for the salvation of souls.

When Lucia was being scoffed at and treated with. contempt in her native village, she decided not to go to the Cova da Iria to meet Our Lady on the 13th of July. It was Jacinta, together with her brother Francisco, who remained firm in her determination to go there. «Francisco and I are going», she said, in tears, «and I shall speak to Our Lady myself». Later, all three joyfully embraced each other, for Lucia had changed her mind and was resolved to go with them.

On the evening of the first apparition, 13th May 1917, despite all her promises to Lucia not to say anything about the apparition, Jacinta told her mother everything: «Mother», she said, «I saw Our Lady today in the Cova da Iria! Oh, what a beautiful Lady!». It was to Jacinta only that were granted two visions of the Holy Father. She beheld a Pope who was suffering deeply on account of persecutions of the Church, besides wars and destruction which were throwing the world into confusion. «Poor Holy Father!» she said, «we must pray very much for him». From then on, the Pope was always included in the prayers and sacrifices of the little shepherds, especially in those of Jacinta.

After having seen the Immaculate Heart of Mary, Jacinta became intensely de-

The first picture of the three little shepherds, taken on the 13th of July 1917. From the left to the right: Lucia, Francisco and Jacinta.

Lucia's family: In the foreground, seated, is her mother, Maria Rosa dos Santos, with Lucia by her side. The picture was taken after the death of Lucia's father, Antonio dos Santos.

voted to it. She often repeated: «Sweet Heart of Mary, be my salvation!» adding: «I so love the Immaculate Heart of Mary! It is the Heart of our dear Mother in heaven. Sweet Heart of Mary, convert sinners, save souls from hell... If only I could put into the hearts of all the fire that is burning within my own heart, and that makes me love the Hearts of Jesus and Mary so very much!»

To save souls from the fires of hell, she spared herself no sacrifice. She refused to drink water in the heat of summer, she gave away her lunch to children poorer than herself, she endured the torture of a piece of rope tied tightly round her waist, with three knots pressing against her tender skin, she underwent exhausting interrogations, and she patiently bore the insults meted out to her by many people. She did all this without the slightest complaint. «I'm so sorry for sinners!» she would say. «If only I could show them hell! How happy I would be if they could all go to heaven!». About a year after the apparitions, Jacinta entered upon the way of the cross that was to lead to her death. After bronchial pneumonia, a purulent abscess formed in the pleura, which caused her acute pain. She was taken to the Hospital of Vila Nova de Ourém. She saw in this a new opportunity to suffer for the conversion of sinners. Two months later, she returned home, with an open wound in the side. Tuberculosis was inexorably consuming her small emaciated body. She was suffering for Our Lord, and asked Lucia: 'Will Jesus be pleased with the offering of my sufferings?»

In February 1920, Jacinta was taken to another hospital, this time in Lisbon. Certain as she was that she would die alone without her parents or Lucia, she found comfort in the thought that this was another opportunity of suffering for sinners. In that hospital, Jacinta was favoured with three visits from Our Lady. While there, the little girl uttered words of wisdom far beyond her age, both as to their delivery and their content, and upon the most varied subjects. She spoke of priests, statesmen, doctors, persecutors of the Church, the obedience of religious, matrimony, riches, poverty... These were surely ideas that came from above.

Finally, on the night of the 20th of February, 1920, the promise of the «Lady brighter than the sun» was fulfilled: «I shall come to take you to heaven», she had said.

Jacinta was buried in the cemetery of Vila Nova de Ourém, and later, in 1935, in the Fatima parish cemetery. On March 1st, 1951, her mortal remains still pre-

Lucia, clothed in the habit of a Dorothean Sister, with the Bishop of Leiria, Dom José Alves Correira da Silva.

The well in the garden of Lucia's family, where the Angel appeared for the second time.

served, were placed in a side-chape to the left of the high altar of the Fatima Basilica. The process for the beatification of the two little seers, Jacinta and Francisco, has been concluded. They will be beatified in springtime of the year 2000.

Lucia

She was born on the 22nd of March, 1907, daughter of Antonio dos Santos and Maria Rosa. She was a cousin of Francisco and Jacinta, the youngest of seven children and the eldest of the little shepherds. She was particularly fond of children and knew how to win their affection. Vivacious by temperament and of a lively intelligence, she was accustomed to organize games, dances, prayers and other initiatives for the children of the village.

Her troubles began after the first apparition of Our Lady. She became the main target of attack for the villagers and even members of her own family. The parish priest suggested that «it might be a trick of the devil». She reached the point of deciding not to keep her appointment with Our Lady on the 13th of July, 1917; but later, acting on a supernatural impulse, and encouraged by her cousins' insistence, she went along with them. Another cause of great suffering

Above: The house of the family Antonio dos Santos, where Lucia was born.

Below: the house of Manuel Marto, father of Francisco and Jacinta.

for Lucia was that Our Lady told her that she would soon take Jacinta and Francisco to heaven, but that Lucia would remain on earth alone to spread devotion to the Immaculate Heart of Mary. Our Lady comforted her, saying: «My Immaculate Heart will be your refuge and the way that will lead you to God».

It was always Lucia who spoke to Our Lady, who presented to her the petitions of many people, and who asked for a miracle to be performed in order that all might believe in the apparitions. When the little shepherds were imprisoned on the 13th of August 1917, it was Lucia who encouraged their resistance to the threats and flatteries which sought to wrestle from them the secret confided to them by Our Lady.

When Francisco and Jacinta fell ill, Lucia visited them constantly and comforted them with the most tender affection.

In 1921, the Bishop of Leiria arranged for Lucia to leave Aljustrel and be educated by the Dorothean Sisters at Vilar, near Porto. Her presence at Fatima could be an obstacle to impartiality in the investigations about the authenticity of the apparitions. Moreover, Lucia was also constantly exposed to so many tiring interrogations.

Later on, Lucia joined the congregation of the Dorothean Sisters where she took the religious vows in 1928. She remained there until 1948, the year in which she entered the Carmel of St. Therese at Coimbra.

There she made her profession in the following year and received the name of Sr. Lucia of the Immaculate Heart of Mary. She died in that same convent on the 13th of February 2005, and was buried in the cemetery of the sisters. But on the 19th of February 2006, her mortal remains were translated to Fatima and buried in the Basilica of the Shrine, in a tomb beside that of Blessed Jacinta.

Lucia lived moments of great joy when Pope Paul VI came to Fatima to be present at the ceremonies marking the 50th anniversary of the apparitions, on the 13th of May 1967. Lucia was also in Fatima on the 13th of May 2000. It is easy to guess what she felt in her heart, when Pope John Paul II beatified her cousins Francisco and Jacinta.

This is the brief history of the three little shepherds of Fatima: of Francisco, the contemplative, ever eager to console Our Lord; of Jacinta, who so deeply loved the Immaculate Heart of Mary and was always looking for new ways of making sacrifices for the conversion of sinners; and of Lucia, the apostle of the Blessed Virgin, who stayed such a long time on earth to spread the message of Fatima.

On the right, above: the bed in which Francisco died. ▷

Below: the roomm where Francisco and Jacinta were born. ▷

The Bishop of Leiria-Fatima, D. Serafim Ferreira e Silva, welcomes the Holy Father.

The Basilica of Fatima, with the images of Francisco and Jacinta, on the day of their beatification.

BEATIFICATION OF FRANCISCO AND JACINTA

On 12 and 13 May 2000, year of the Jubilee, Pope John Paul II visited Fatima for the third time. During the Mass which took place on 13 May, the pope beatified Francisco and Jacinta Marto, beginning his homily with these words: «Bless You, Father, for you hid these truths from the wise and knowing, and revealed them to children». Regarding the significance of the beatification of the two little shepherds, he said: «With this ritual, the Church places in its candelabrum these two candles which God lighted that they might illuminate humanity in its time of darkness and doubt».

The beatification of Francisco and Jacinta is, then, the Church's confirmation of the credibility of the apparitions at Fatima, and recognition that these children are a model for young and old alike. The lives of these two blessed children was devoted to giving their love to sinners, the sick and the poor in the form of prayer, gifts of food, visits and words of consolation and guidance.

JUBILEU 2000 · DEUS FEZ-SE HOMEM EM MARIA

John Paul II praying beside the tombs of Francisco and Jacinta.

Third part of the «Secret»

At the end of the Mass for the beatification of Francisco and Jacinta, Cardinal Angelo Sodano, Vatican Secretary of State, announced to the thousands of pilgrims at the Cova da Iria that the Holy Father had entrusted the Congregation for the Doctrine of the Faith with the task of making public the text of the third part of the «Secret of Fatima». The text of this third part of the Secret, written by Sister Lucia on 3 January 1944 and made public on 26 June 2000, in Rome, is as follows:
«J.M.J.

The third part of the secret revealed at the Cova da Iria-Fatima, on 13 July 1917. I write in obedience to you, my God, who command me to do so through his Excellency the Bishop of Leiria and through your Most Holy Mother and mine.

After the two parts which I have already explained, at the left of Our Lady and a little above, we saw an Angel with a flaming sword in his left hand; flashing, it gave out flames that looked as though they would set the world on fire; but they died out in contact with the splendour that Our Lady radiated towards him from her right hand: pointing to the earth with his right hand, the Angel cried out in a loud voice: 'Penance, Penance, Penance!'. And we saw in an immense light that is God: 'something similar to how people appear in a mirror when they pass in front of it' a Bishop dressed in White 'we had the impression that it was the Holy Father'. Other Bishops, Priests, men and women Religious going up a steep mountain, at the top of which there was a big Cross of rough-hewn trunks as of a cork-tree with the bark; before reaching there the Holy Father passed through a big city half in ruins

Sister Lucía took part in the Mass for the beatification of her cousins, and later visited the places where the Angel and Our Lady appeared the little shepherd children.

and half trembling with halting step, afflicted with pain and sorrow, he prayed for the souls of the corpses he met on his way; having reached the top of the mountain, on his knees at the foot of the big Cross he was killed by a group of soldiers who fired bullets and arrows at him, and in the same way there died one after another the other Bishops, Priests, men and women Religious, and various lay people of different ranks and positions. Beneath the two arms of the Cross there were two Angels each with a crystal aspersorium in his hand, in which they gathered up the blood of the Martyrs and with it sprinkled the souls that were making their way to God. Tuy-3-1-1944».

CONTENTS

BIBLIOGRAPHY

Ir. Lucia do Coração I maculado, Memória e escritos, Fátima 1978.
Visconde de Montelo (pseud.) Manuel Nunes Formigão, Os Episódios maravilhosos de Fátima, Guarda 1921.
Idem, As grandes maravilhas de Fátima, Guarda 1927.
L. Gonzaga da Fonseca, Nossa Senhora de Fátima, 1934.
Idem in italiano, Le meraviglie di Fatima, Casale Monferrato 1942, IV ediz.
Antero de Figueiredo, Fátima, Graças, Segredo, Mistérios, Lisboa 1936.
J. De Marchi, Era uma Senhora mais brilhante que o sol, Fáti ma 1946,111 ed.
Costa Brochado, Fátima à luz da História, Lisboa 1948.
S. Martins dos Reis, Fátima, as suas provas e osseus problemas, Lisboa 1953.
L.M. Fisher, Fatima, das portugiesische Lourdes, Baden 1930.
Ch. Barthas, Fátima merveille du XXe siecle, Toulouse 1953.
Finbar Ryan, Our Lady of Fatima, Dublin 1939.
António Maria Martins, Documentos de Fátima, Porto 1976.

PHOTOGRAPHS

Archives of the Sanctuary of Fatima
FISA – Escudo de Oro
Arturo Mari

EDITORIAL ESCUDO DE ORO, S.A.
I.S.B.N. 972-8265-08-5
Editorial Fisa Escudo de Oro, S.A.
Veneçuela, 105 - 08019 Barcelona
Legal Dep. B. 9459-2006